IMAGES OF NATURE

MISSOURI

CHARLES GURCHE

FOREWORD BY THOMAS EAGLETON

WESTCLIFFE PUBLISHERS, INC. ENGLEWOOD, COLORADO

CONTENTS

International Standard Book Number:
   ISBN 0-929969-31-6
Library of Congress Catalogue Card Number: 89-52039
Copyright, Photographs and Text: Charles Gurche, 1990.
   All rights reserved.
Editor: John Fielder
Assistant Editor: Margaret Terrell Morse
Production Manager: Mary Jo Lawrence
Typographer: Dianne J. Borneman
Printed in Korea by Sung In Printing Company, Ltd.,
   Seoul
Published by Westcliffe Publishers, Inc.
   2650 South Zuni Street
   Englewood, Colorado 80110

Bibliography

Carpenter, Allan. *Missouri, From Its Glorious Past to the Present.*
   Chicago: Childrens Press, Inc., 1966. Reprinted with permission.
Gusewelle, C.W. *Far from Any Coast: Pieces of America's Heartland.*
   Columbia: University of Missouri Press, 1989. Reprinted with
   permission.
Nagel, Paul C. *Missouri, A Bicentennial History.* New York: W.W.
   Norton & Company, Inc., 1977. Reprinted with permission,
   including the Leonard Hall quotation on p. 108.
Twain, Mark. *The Adventures of Tom Sawyer.* New York: Grosset &
   Dunlap Publishers, 1946.

First Frontispiece: Field of buttercups at sunset,
   Ripley County
Second Frontispiece: Sunset fires barren trees along
   the Missouri River, Pelican Island Natural Area,
   St. Louis County
Title Page: Abstract reflections in the waters of
   Blue Spring, Ozark National Scenic Riverways
Right: Granite boulders frame puffs of clouds,
   Elephant Rocks State Park

THOMAS EAGLETON

FOREWORD

Missouri is the population center of the United States—De Soto, Missouri, just below St. Louis, to be precise. It contains a unique blend of personality and beauty befitting the heart of America. I'll concede that some other state may have a particular scene that would challenge for number one in the American beauty parade, but I'll wager that no state contains the diversity of beauty in such striking abundance as does Missouri. All parts of Missouri make their offerings of exciting, aesthetic pleasure. From incomparable sunrises on the Mississippi River to the mysteries of Onondaga Cave, from swirls in Pickle Creek to the hush of Mark Twain National Forest, Missouri is a resplendent mosaic of nature's gifts.

Everyone has his or her particular place of beauty and serenity. Mine is the Irish Wilderness. When I served in the United States Senate, along with John Karel (now the director of Tower Grove Park in St. Louis) and Rindy O'Brien (now with the Wilderness Society), I worked on the legislation that included the Irish Wilderness in the National Wilderness Preservation System.

Just what is this curiously named Irish Wilderness? A young Irish priest, Father John Hogan, settled this area in southern Missouri in 1858. Deeply affected by the suffering and poverty he saw among his fellow immigrants in the railroad camps around St. Louis, Father Hogan led a group of about 40 families to the wilderness of southern Missouri where they bought government land for 12.5 cents per acre. The settlers picked the wrong time to make their move, for they found themselves to be in no man's land and were besieged by both Confederates and Yankees, as well as bushwhackers. Precisely what happened to them is not known. Thus, the mystery of the Irish immigrants is part of the character of the land today.

Father Hogan's own words provide the most moving description of the area's beauty.

The quiet solitariness of the place seemed to inspire devotion. Nowhere could the human soul so profoundly worship as in the depths of that leafy forest, beneath the swaying branches of the lofty oaks and pines, where solitude and the heart of man united in praise and wonder of the Great Creator.

The original stands of pine and oak were cut down at the end of the 19th century, but the basic forest cover has returned. With each passing year, the Irish, as the old-timers call it, more closely resembles the virgin forest. Its Ozark wildlife—whitetail deer, squirrel, coyote, bobcat, raccoon, rabbit, gray fox—is as varied as it is abundant. The diverse topography, countless wildflowers and propinquity to the free-flowing and unspoiled Eleven Point River—itself set aside as a national scenic river area—make the Irish Wilderness unique in Missouri and the nation. Indeed, it is the crown jewel of the Missouri wilderness system. Its pristine caves, hollows, ridges, bluffs and disappearing streams are breathtaking. Its limestone topography and geological structure draw many students for field examinations. There's nothing quite like it in Missouri—or anywhere else, I submit.

Father Hogan was right. The Irish Wilderness is a place "where solitude and the heart of man united in praise and wonder of the Great Creator."

But enough of *my* favorite. If the Irish Wilderness isn't yours, somewhere else in Missouri will be. Missouri is the Show Me State, but in terms of breadth of beauty, Missouri wants to be the Show You State. As you look through this book, as you examine the incomparable photography of Charles Gurche, you will see why Missouri is one of America's most diverse and captivating hidden treasures.

—THOMAS EAGLETON
U.S. Senator, Missouri, 1969-1987

Old mill wheel at Turner's Mill along the Eleven Point River, at the edge of the Irish Wilderness, Oregon County
Overleaf: Fall forest surrounds Ha Ha Tonka Spring, Ha Ha Tonka State Park

CHARLES GURCHE
PREFACE

The early song of the robin signaled that another Missouri morning had begun. Soon after the first hint of light touched the eastern sky, horizontal bands of color appeared, beginning with a glowing orange on the horizon and layering up to yellow, turquoise, pale blue and deep blue. Dawn dimly illuminated scattered oaks, veiled in a thin fog that had settled in the valleys during the calm night. Purple hills met a crimson sky where the sun would soon appear. With a single stroke, sunrise shattered the pastels of the landscape and replaced them with contrast.

All across the state a new day was beginning. Early light glowed warmly on silos and barns in northern Missouri as shadows stretched across the surrounding fields. In the Ozark Mountains, fog along the riverways turned from blue to gold. Dark silhouettes of ancient cypress trees reflected in the swampy wetlands of Missouri's southeastern corner. On a Missouri River sand bar, the low light illuminated textures and patterns in the sand that had lain hidden moments before. Leaves in every forest shone like glowing fragments of stained glass. Sunlight danced in hundreds of brilliant flashes on ripples in the Eleven Point River. Dew sparkled across the western prairies. The land was new again in the early morning light.

As a child growing up on the outer edge of Kansas City, I had a world of wonder and exploration beyond the borders of my backyard. A small creek ran across a bed of limestone, over a small falls and into a deep pool. Across the creek was an old forest where tall oaks sheltered stony trails leading to secret hideaways. As I roamed about freely, the tiny landscape became a familiar companion.

From my upstairs bedroom window, I could gaze upon this land and observe a continually changing drama. On hot summer nights I watched the lightning bolts of powerful storms illuminate rushing torrents of brown water in the swollen stream. In autumn the canopy of trees became a tapestry of warm color, until a November cold snap exposed the scraggly skeletons of oaks on the hillside. Winter's rare and treasured snowfalls transformed the land into a scene of quiet purity. In spring the woods blossomed with purples and greens, life returned to the pools in the creek, and the trill of frogs was music to sleep by. My backyard was a rich introduction to the spirit of these lands.

Summer trips exposed me to the multitude of creeks and woods farther from home. My first journey to the Ozarks revealed an immense land which seemed incredibly wild and great and pure. The streams were crystal clear, the hills towering, the forests endless. I wanted to be everywhere at once. There were simply too many caves to explore, too many rivers to float, too many rocks to climb.

At 18 I left for college in the West. Despite the grand scale and beauty of this new landscape, I never forgot the special power of Missouri's lands. You can feel it in the forest on a fall afternoon when leaves rustle underfoot and crows and blackbirds call from a distant cornfield. You can feel it in the silence after a white blanket of snow has quieted the land. You can feel it on a mild March day when the sun warms your body and the rich smells of the earth return once again. You can feel it on the open prairie when a dark thunderstorm approaches and the tremendous power of distant thunder breaks the stillness of a summer afternoon.

When I returned to Missouri as a professional photographer, many childhood memories were rekindled as I rediscovered the streams and forests I had known years before. One summer evening I explored the extensive sand bars of Pelican Island on the Missouri River near St. Louis. Lonely driftwood snags gave the desertlike landscape a primal feeling as the setting sun cast an amber light on the land. There was a magical childhood timelessness to the scene, as though Tom Sawyer were calling me to feel the sand with my bare feet and sit by a fire long into the night. The essence of summer lay about the land.

Five months later, on a frigid December morning, my father and I set out in darkness to meet the sunrise at Lake Jacomo. Snow had fallen the previous day, and at

Hoarfrost on eastern cottonwoods, Jackson County

15 degrees below zero, eerie plumes of steam rose from the lake. As the light of day brightened I quickly scouted for a good spot to capture the mood. A lone oak stood silhouetted against the fog, and the fine light of the rising sun soon created a mystical scene. It was a photographer's dream and a unique slice of time that we felt lucky to have witnessed.

People as well as places stand out in my mind as I think back on the eight trips I took through Missouri while photographing for this book. Help and encouragement were freely given, as well as directions to remote locations and permission to photograph on private land. Mechanics arrived from nowhere when my car failed, and most everyone had at least one idea of a spot for a great picture. The assistance and goodwill I encountered everywhere were very appreciated and were essential ingredients of this book.

My never-ending question as I traveled the state was how to truly capture the strong attachment that I feel for the Missouri landscape. At the end of one very good day of photography, I finally just stopped. I stopped thinking about strong compositions and capturing the light at its best. I stopped rushing to set up my view camera and then rushing off to set it up again in a new spot while the light was still good. I could tell it was time to stop. My last shot had been of a full moon in a twilight sky, rising above the vast boulders at Elephant Rocks. Work for the day was finished.

I sat down on a huge boulder overlooking the landscape. I was alone. In the stillness of the evening, my senses became more aware. Sights and sounds were simple and few, yet this seemed to give the night a special power. As twilight deepened, silver moonlight began to cast shadows at the bases of the standing boulders. Far off in the dark woods the silence was broken by a great horned owl that called out and was answered by another. Silence returned once again. I stared out at the moon, the rocks and the forests beyond, hoping that the picture I had taken earlier would tell some of the story of the richness of this night or at least serve as an invitation for others to go out and sit before a rising moon.

The images presented in this book were created by searching for the beautiful, the wild and the unaltered natural world of Missouri. Yet, over the years, many places in the state have not fared as well. Miles and miles of cypress wetlands that once teemed with wildlife were deemed useless many years ago and the land drained and cut. Less than 1 percent of the state's once-extensive tallgrass prairie remains today. Virgin, old-growth forests are extremely rare, and pollution has marred rivers and streams. Scarce plant and animal species continue to decline in number, and beautiful, ancient formations have been vandalized in numerous caves. Missouri's undisturbed natural areas have become even more valuable in their rareness.

We owe much to the energies of those insightful people who have worked to preserve Missouri's remaining natural treasures. Many wild lands are now protected in state parks, wilderness areas, national riverways, designated natural areas and private holdings. These lands provide sanctuary for plant and animal life and ensure that the special value of wildness will always endure in Missouri.

Still, many pristine areas remain unprotected and vulnerable to destruction. They need our support for their preservation. Protection of the lands we are blessed with will preserve a quality of life for every following generation. Missouri's fragile beauty rests solely on our values and actions, for we are the stewards of a precious and irreplaceable land.

—CHARLES GURCHE

For their continuous encouragement and support, I dedicate this book to my parents, Suzanne and John C. Gurche, and to my wife, Sara Ashley Devins.

Eroded limestone and Tower Rock, Mississippi River

COLOR

Part of the joy of looking at the natural world lies in the delight of viewing endless displays of color. Infinite variety can be found, from bold primary hues to soft pastels to shades of brown and gray. All have the potential to evoke emotional responses in the viewer. Sometimes the power of color is obvious and overwhelming; at other times it subtly alters our subconscious moods.

Just as the natural world is in a constant state of change, so are its rich varieties and combinations of color. Seasons and other cycles of life and the changing light throughout each day continually alter the colors of stone, water, plant and sky.

Nature's colors have a vital connection to the impact of my photography. When I am out in the field, I often search for a special quality of color or combination of tones that might heighten visual awareness or create a sense of wonder for our natural lands. During my recent travels in Missouri, I sought out the warm tones of light early and late in the day, the cool colors of the springs and the bright hues of the vegetation. I was continually delighted by new tones and combinations of color that revealed themselves in the landscape.

Left: White oak trunk and watercress at Blue Spring, Ozark National Scenic Riverways   Above: Sunset reflection on pond, Jefferson County

"Many of the state's rivers are fed by springs. In fact, probably no state surpasses Missouri in the number of large springs." — Allan Carpenter

Wintry scene at Ha Ha Tonka Spring, Ha Ha Tonka State Park

Duckweed patterns at Mingo National Wildlife Refuge, Wayne County

"[The spring's] basin was encrusted with a frostwork of glittering crystals; it was in the midst of a cavern whose walls were supported . . . by the joining of great stalactites and stalagmites together, the result of the ceaseless water-drip of centuries." — Mark Twain

Bald cypress and water tupelo rise up from the waters of Otter Slough Natural Area, Stoddard County

Limestone formations, Onondaga Cave State Park

Prairie coneflowers in bloom, James A. Reed Memorial Wildlife Area, Jackson County

Lichens and hanging plants on Buzzard's Bluff, St. Clair County

"[After the fires] spring rains flushed off the ash, and the topsoil with it, into streams running milky gray out of their banks. The first fine grass came, then birdfoot violets."
— C.W. Gusewelle

Deep, cold waters of Alley Spring, Ozark National Scenic Riverways

Bird-foot violets nestle among white oak leaves, Mark Twain National Forest, Stone County
Overleaf: October forest and fields along the Current River, Ozark National Scenic Riverways

"Just as the interior of the region had forbidden heavy Indian occupation, so it would support only a thin salting of white settlers, and to travel the area even now is to understand why. Civilization moved principally by water, and many of the rivers of the Ozarks were only seasonably, if ever, navigable." — C.W. Gusewelle

Red Mill reflects in Alley Spring, Ozark National Scenic Riverways, Shannon County

Fall reflections on Pickle Creek, Hawn State Park

"Ahead and below, the waves of broken land run off to blueness under a haze of wood smoke. . . . [These hills are] full of bugs and snakes and fires in season, and empty dark. And they could be forbidding except that now, with spring's advance, they are washed a luminous green. The dogwood is out, the redbud just finishing." — C.W. Gusewelle

Snow-covered fields stretch to the horizon, Randolph County

Flowering dogwood, Irish Wilderness

"Steep hillsides were densely timbered, often shallowly underlain by rock. Through the rest of the nineteenth century the main body of western settlement would push through and around the highlands." — C.W. Gusewelle

Eroded sandstone of Double Arch, Pickle Springs Natural Area

Sugar maples at sunrise, Marion County

"The Ozark highlands are changing, and *must* change. But it is not unreasonable to hope that, in the process, something of the character and values of the highlands might endure. For, in that country, enduring is a practiced art." — C.W. Gusewelle

Branches silhouetted against Round Spring, Ozark National Scenic Riverways

Vegetation casts long shadows on a Missouri River sand bar, St. Louis County

FORM

The French painter Claude Monet once stated that in order to see, we must forget the name of the thing we are looking at. Our view of the landscape before us then becomes a blend of straight and curved lines, light and dark forms, textures, patterns and shapes. When this happens a vision of pure form is allowed to surface.

Nature abounds with every shape and design imaginable. At first glance our world may seem visually cluttered and chaotic. To lend visual impact to a photograph of the natural world, some type of selecting and simplifying must occur. Seeing purely in terms of form is one of the best ways to strengthen the visual design of a photograph. Dynamic shapes, patterns and lines can then be emphasized in the composition of the image.

The upside-down image on the ground glass of a view camera is actually an asset to seeing design and form. It enables the photographer to lose the standard way of looking at the world and to begin a process of reducing a scene down to its essential components of form. The result is often a powerful image that presents a new dimension of an ordinary subject or creates a different awareness or curiosity toward the subject.

Left: Water tupelo trees cast shadows across pollen-covered waters in Cupola Pond Natural Area, Mark Twain National Forest, Ripley County
Above: Vines above Blue Spring, Laclede County

"The time was early January. The hour, that numb, hollow-stomached one between night and morning. The temperature had fallen and what rattled now like birdshot against the windshield . . . was a mongrel wetness, neither sleet nor rain." — *C.W. Gusewelle*

Sunrise silhouettes lone oak on a sub-zero morning at Lake Jacomo, Jackson County

Gnarled branches of a 140-foot bur oak, Big Oak Tree State Park, Mississippi County

Last light of day at Pelican Island Natural Area on the Missouri River, St. Louis County

Reeds in pond at sunrise, St. Clair County
Overleaf: Sunrise at Tower Rock Natural Area on the Mississippi River, Perry County

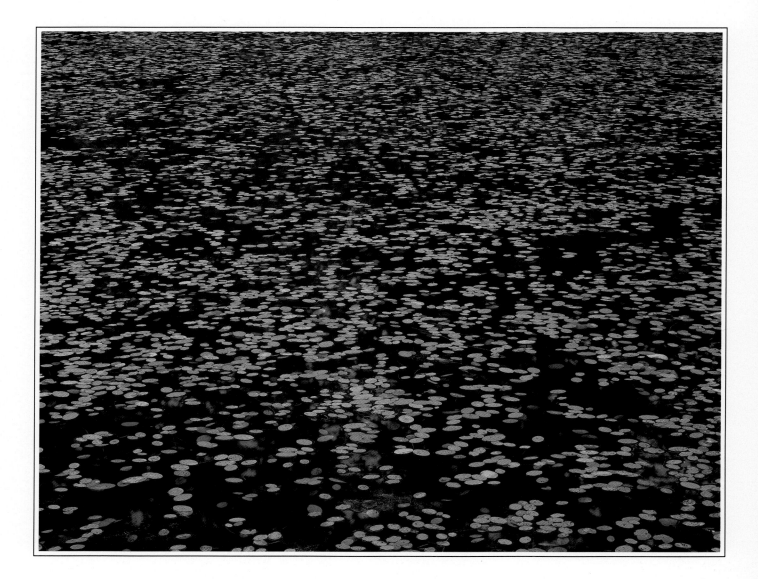

"Certainly if completeness was the measure, nature intended Missouri as another Eden. . . . The variety of the state's geography and resources hinted at a wholeness worthy of the original Paradise. She had vast woodlands, including what would become two national forests." — Paul C. Nagel

Water shield leaves dot surface of Loggers Lake, Mark Twain National Forest, Shannon County

Water shield leaves punctuate tree reflections on Little Scotia Pond, Mark Twain National Forest, Dent County

"In ancient times most of what is now Missouri was buried beneath age-old seas again and again, only to rise once more. Sometimes mountain ranges raised their heights and then were worn away over the centuries. They too sometimes rose again, only to be worn off once more." — Allan Carpenter

Setting sun illuminates granite potholes, Elephant Rocks State Park, Iron County

Black oak leaf on lichen-covered boulder, St. Francois County

"Missouri was said to have been particularly blessed by nature . . . as if the Mississippi River divided the nation into two great communities, with the newer portion being much grander and more promising than the eastern region—the mountains and rivers in the East looked puny beside those of the West." — Paul C. Nagel

Morning shadows on snow-blanketed Sons Creek, Dade County

"... wide interest in her natural wealth and prominence
encouraged Missourians to believe in their state's universal
strength, for who could deny that nature had dealt generously
with the state, leaving handsome bequests of marvelous land,
river valleys, forests, mineral deposits, and helpful weather?"

— Paul C. Nagel

Farmer's contoured fields, Platte County

"On the hill behind are the remains of a dwelling, home of the master of Tigris overlooking his fief, consumed on a winter night by some accident with the flue. A mansion it was, judging by the size of the footings." — C.W. Gusewelle

Natural fissures of Castle Rock, Madison County

Dusting of snow on eastern red cedars and Ha Ha Tonka castle remains, Ha Ha Tonka State Park

"The forest, when first man saw it, was an oak and hickory climax, with the native shortleaf pine interspersed in pockets. ... The look of such a hardwood forest can only be imagined now. The great leaf crowns interlaced above in a canopy that blocked the sun, retarding undergrowth." — C.W. Gusewelle

White oaks and shortleaf pines on spring hillside, Shannon County

Lichens decorate granite boulders and black oak, Elephant Rocks State Park

MOMENT

Everything in nature is in the midst of continuous transition. If viewed closely, time-lapse photography focused on a single piece of land would show thousands of changes occurring each day and millions during the course of a year. Leaves and blossoms would grow, turn color, fall and decay. Fog, rain and snow would take turns altering the scene. The changing light throughout each day would steadily affect the form and color of the landscape. What we sometimes think of as static images of nature are actually unique slices of time in a constantly changing drama.

Certain moments in time seem to possess a power to express the harmony, spirit and beauty of the natural world. These often brief moments allow us to see, think and feel with greater awareness. The fresh greens of early spring, the glistening frost of winter, the golden glow of a setting sun, the blanket of fog at daybreak—all are moments that capture the strong spirit of the land.

While traveling through Missouri, I attempted to capture a wide range of fascinating slices of time that would communicate the many personalities of the landscape. I tried to anticipate moments of peak energy, delicate beauty and magic. Each photograph that resulted from this effort shows just one image selected from a changing natural world. Together they tell a story of the passage of time.

Left: Early morning in the Ozark Mountains, Mark Twain National Forest, Carter County   Above: Barns at sunrise, Lewis County

Fresh snow in forest, Jackson County

Sunrise on Longview Lake, Jackson County   Overleaf: Morning mists and farmer's fields, Holt County

"... the sun has revealed itself, without warmth, shining through a sudden shower of snow crystals blown on the cutting wind." — C.W. Gusewelle

New-fallen snow on barn at Missouri Town 1855, Fleming Park, Jackson County

"The sky has gone curdy gray, spilling wind. It has been seven weeks since a decent rain." — C.W. Gusewelle

Storm clouds fill the sky above a farmer's fields, Jasper County

"Bagnell Dam . . . backed up the Osage to create the Lake of the Ozarks. . . . The impact of these reservoirs has been mixed. They brought construction money, and later tourist money, into the region. They also drowned tillable valley acres, swallowed communities, and displaced thousands of Ozarkers. . . ." — C.W. Gusewelle

White oak and granite boulders silhouetted in sunset's afterglow, Elephant Rocks State Park

Buttonbush reflected at sunrise, Lake of the Ozarks, Camden County

"The cold in the valley has begun to bite. Fog from the stream has billowed up to the base of the fence below the lane, receded once, and now is rolling up again." — *C.W. Gusewelle*

Whisper of a barn on a foggy morning, Ste. Genevieve County

Eastern red cedars at sunset, Madison County

"But one of the principal resources, replenishable, if at all, only over the course of a century or more, had been the hardwood forest. When it was gone, and the timber companies gone with it, the people left behind . . . were a people the burgeoning nation had forgotten." — C.W. Gusewelle

Sunrise warms historic Fort Osage, Jackson County

Oak forest in morning fog, Mark Twain National Forest, Carter County

"Missouri's natural glory was first beheld from the rivers. The pioneers, whether farmers or traders, joined the rivermen in thinking of Missouri as land lying along marvelous, even awesome river pathways." — Paul C. Nagel

Boulders punctuate the still waters of the St. Francis River, Madison County

"The night was far spent. It was broad daylight before [Tom Sawyer] found himself fairly abreast the island bar. He rested again until the sun was well up and gilding the great river with its splendor, and then he plunged into the stream."

— Mark Twain

Tower Rock shields the rising sun, Mississippi River, Perry County

PLACE

Sometimes a fine landscape photograph gives viewers the feeling that they can step right into the picture. Foreground details may appear close enough to touch, giving the image a three-dimensional sensation.

An image with a strong sense of place is usually made from a unique perspective. Low camera placement and interesting foreground detail produce a photograph with an impression of extended depth. In the lily pad image to the left, for instance, the camera was on a tripod that had been submerged four feet into swampy water and mud. I was in a canoe behind the tripod, working the camera and trying to hold still enough to eliminate any ripples on the surface of the water.

Missouri stands at the crossroads of eastern woodlands, central prairies and southern wetlands. Geologic forces have added a fine assortment of unusual features to the landscape, and the seasons are distinct and pure. The images in this book only scratch the surface of showing the many fabulous places in the state.

Left: Lily pads in Otter Slough Natural Area, Stoddard County
Above: Native grasslands at sunrise, Niawathe Prairie Natural Area, Dade County

Sheer limestone bluff looms above Lake of the Ozarks, Ha Ha Tonka State Park

Mustard in bloom, Bollinger County
Overleaf: Sunrise along the shore of Table Rock Lake, Mark Twain National Forest, Stone County

"From there, with the country spread out below, you can observe the larger pattern of change.
The bulldozers have been at work. The woodland has diminished. The farm fields have grown larger and more regular, and young men . . . drive across those fields on tractors whose cost was greater than the price of the farm."
— C.W. Gusewelle

Rolled hay bales, Platte County

Duckweed and leaves cluster on the surface of Ha Ha Tonka Spring, Ha Ha Tonka State Park

"Within this extent . . . lay Missouri's wondrous river system, which her citizens especially cherished. Missourians knew from the beginning how important the Mississippi and Missouri rivers had made their state. They contended that the Missouri River was the longest and most powerful stream in the world, leaving the Mississippi its tributary." — Paul C. Nagel

Mossy boulders in the swift-moving waters of Greer Spring, Oregon County

Evening light on a Missouri River sand bar, St. Louis County

Looking down from Buzzard's Bluff to the Sac River, St. Clair County

Rock Bridge frames a branch of the Little Bonne Femme Creek, Rock Bridge Memorial State Park

Whirlpool and falls on Pickle Creek, Hawn State Park

View from the top of Rocky Falls, Ozark National Scenic Riverways

MICROCOSM

When we take the time to notice subtle details of the landscape, we open ourselves to an appreciation and awareness of a different scale of beauty around us. An inner world of leaves, flowers, grasses, ice, water and stone blends in endless combinations of form and color. Observing this closeup world reveals the relationships in nature to be an interconnected web of life.

Looking at our immediate surroundings in the natural world tends to free the vision, allowing us to see things purely for their design elements. Subjects lose their reality and become observed shapes, lines, patterns and colors. There is great freedom in composition, as movements of the camera and choices of what to include or omit greatly alter each image. As a result, the photographer can strengthen the basic elements of design inherent in the natural world.

During the two years I spent creating images for this collection, I often observed details of the landscape that told a seasonal story. My best photographs often showed subjects in an important seasonal transition of their life span. Sometimes I would become so involved in looking at the scene and manipulating the camera that later I would be surprised to realize I had been working in one small area for two or three hours.

Left: White oak and flowering dogwood leaves in Little Scotia Pond, Mark Twain National Forest, Dent County
Above: Watercress in Alley Spring, Ozark National Scenic Riverways

Frost crystals build on the icy surface of Sons Creek, Dade County

Water shield leaves accented by white oak and flowering dogwood leaves, Dent County

Ice formations on mossy rocks, Hickory Canyons Natural Area, Ste. Genevieve County

Water shield leaves and stems on Little Scotia Pond, Mark Twain National Forest, Dent County
Overleaf: Moss-covered boulders form rapids in Bennett Spring, Bennett Spring State Park, Dallas County

Red maple leaves and lichens on boulders, Paddy Creek Wilderness

Musk thistle seeds cushion solitary grass stalk, Jackson County

Water ripples over stones in Shut-in Creek, Bell Mountain Wilderness, Mark Twain National Forest, Iron County

Azalea blossoms, reindeer moss and black oak leaves, Hawn State Park

"Prairie flowers still include many described by C.J. Latrobe in 1832: 'God has here with a prodigal hand scattered the seeds of thousands of beautiful plants.' " — Allan Carpenter

Indian paintbrush blooms amid prairie grasses, Prairie State Park

Reflections and shadows of water tupelo trees, Cupola Pond Natural Area, Mark Twain National Forest, Ripley County

Red maple leaves along Pickle Creek, Hawn State Park

Black tupelo and cattails, Iron County

LIGHT

Light is the single most important influence on our vision of the natural world and our emotional response to it. Light has the power to illuminate texture, produce contrast, alter color and create design, shape and pattern.

The power of light lies in its many personalities. Light varies throughout each day in its intensity, color and direction. Each of these properties can be used to amplify the power of a photograph and affect our view of a scene.

Light usually determined where, when and how I photographed in Missouri. On clear days I usually gravitated to open areas where the direct rays of the sun could give their full impact. A backlit scene took on a dramatic feeling with high contrast, silhouettes and great depth. Side lighting emphasized the forms and textures of a subject. Front lighting at sunrise and sunset added warmth, while the subtle pastels of dawn and dusk gave a mystical feeling to scenes.

The even glow on overcast days provided an excellent white light which was very fine for forest subjects. Details were more apparent and colors often richer in the absence of glaring sunlight and dark shadows. Most of my closeup and midrange scenes were taken under this type of soft light.

Matching my subject with the right light was my primary goal in planning most of the photographs in this book. The best matches resulted in the greatest expressions of the splendor of Missouri's lands.

Left: Full moon above granite boulders, Elephant Rocks State Park
Above: Barns at sunset, Cooper County

"When the choicest float streams were threatened by still more projected dams, conservation groups generated a successful move . . . to preserve them unchanged as National Scenic Rivers." — C.W. Gusewelle

Sparkling clear waters of Big Spring, the largest single-outlet spring in the world, Ozark National Scenic Riverways, Carter County

Pools on a Missouri River sand bar after sunset, St. Louis County

"... much of Missouri appears to be rugged and mountainous. This is due largely to what is known as 'high local relief.' The mountains rise abruptly from their bases to considerable height so that there is great contrast in elevation between a stream valley and a nearby bluff or hill." — Allan Carpenter

Igneous rock on Hughes Mountain in evening light, Hughes Mountain Natural Area, Washington County

Rocks sparkle with spray from Mina Sauk Falls, Mark Twain National Forest, Iron County
Overleaf: Rising sun lights covered bridge and gristmill on the Whitewater River, Bollinger Mill State Historic Site

" . . . one early traveler wrote of the Ozark region: 'The country abounded in millions of deer, turkeys, bear, wolves and small animals. I remember . . . that we could see deer feeding in great herds on the hills like cattle, and wild turkeys were in abundance . . . while furs and hides served as currency of the country.' " — Allan Carpenter

Light of dawn on cypress and water tupelo, Otter Slough Natural Area, Stoddard County

Thistles backlit by setting sun, Jackson County

"*S*ince there is general agreement as to Indian tribes met and types of landscape traversed, there seems little reason to doubt that De Soto and his band . . . reached their 'farthest north' among the granitic knobs of the St. Francois Mountains in what is now Iron County." — Leonard Hall

Late afternoon light on granite boulders, Elephant Rocks State Park, Iron County

"This, then, is . . . hard, decent country—open and fair to
any man, no matter how he talks or looks.
But a country, also, acquainted with disappointment. Where
some men stay for want of hoping . . . and others come home
from what they meant to be. Where towns die and dreams
with them. Where a soul's salvation is near, but fleet afoot.
Where the rain never quite comes in time." — C.W. Gusewelle

Polished rhyolite along the East Fork of the Black River, Johnson's Shut-Ins State Park

Twilight on snow at Mo-Ko Prairie, Cedar County

Red maple and oak leaves, Cuivre River State Park, Lincoln County

Technical Information

The photographic images in this book were made with a Calumet 4x5 view camera on Fujichrome 50 and Ektachrome 64, 100 Plus and 200 films. Fujinon, Nikkor and Schneider lenses were used in focal lengths of 90mm, 150mm, 300mm and 600mm. Shutter speeds ranged from 1/250 second to 90 seconds. Lens apertures varied from f/8 to f/64. Warming filters (81A and 81B) were used in some shaded conditions. A polarizing filter helped reduce glare and increase color saturation.

Acknowledgements

For their kind encouragement and assistance, I am very grateful to Suzanne Gurche, John C. Gurche, Carolyn Gurche, Eugene Jablonsky, Melanie Jablonsky, Marny Gaylord, Randy Gaylord, Dorothy Tolford and the many other friends whose support has made this book possible. I am especially thankful for the great inspiration and vision from my brother, John A. Gurche.

For their help with this project and their work to preserve Missouri's natural lands, I am indebted to many people from the Missouri Department of Natural Resources, Missouri Department of Conservation, Ozark National Scenic Riverways, Mark Twain National Forest, Missouri Prairie Foundation, Missouri Chapter of the Nature Conservancy, Ozark Chapter of the Sierra Club, Conservation Foundation of Missouri, Coalition for the Environment and Audubon Society of Missouri.

I thank Freeman Patterson for sharing—through his words and images—his wonderful spirit and knowledge of photography. Finally, I am ever grateful to the patience and understanding of Sara Devins.

— C.G.

Foggy morning on the Jacks Fork River,
Ozark National Scenic Riverways